SKETCHES OF
AMERINDIAN TRIBES

Sketches
in
BRITISH GUIANA
by
E. A. Goodall.

SKETCHES OF AMERINDIAN TRIBES

1841–1843

by

EDWARD A. GOODALL

with an Introduction and Notes by
M. N. MENEZES

Published by
BRITISH MUSEUM PUBLICATIONS LIMITED
for
THE NATIONAL COMMISSION
FOR RESEARCH MATERIALS ON GUYANA

ISBN 0 7141 0497 3

Published by British Museum Publications Ltd
6 Bedford Square, London WC1B 3RA

Designed by John Mitchell

Phototypeset in 11/13pt Plantin Light by Tradespools Ltd, Frome, Somerset
Printed in Great Britain by Balding & Mansell Ltd, Wisbech, Cambridgeshire

*To the Amerindians of Guyana to whom we owe
a cultural debt, not yet fully appreciated,
this work is specially dedicated.*

CONTENTS

INTRODUCTION

But for yellow fever, the name of Edward Alfred Goodall might never have been known to Guyana, and the nation would have been culturally poorer without his remarkable and realistic water-colour sketches of the Amerindian tribes, their types of dwellings, and his landscapes of the interior of the country. The sketches reproduced in this volume are taken mainly from his collection of approximately eighty sketches of the Amerindian tribes of Guyana: the Warrau and Carib, Arecuna, Wapisiana and Macusi, as well as tribes now extinct in the territory, the Maiongkong, Atorai, Amaripa, Maopityan or Frog Indians, the Pianoghotto, and the Drio Indians.

University of Guyana
Georgetown, Guyana
27 December 1975

M. N. Menezes, R.S.M.

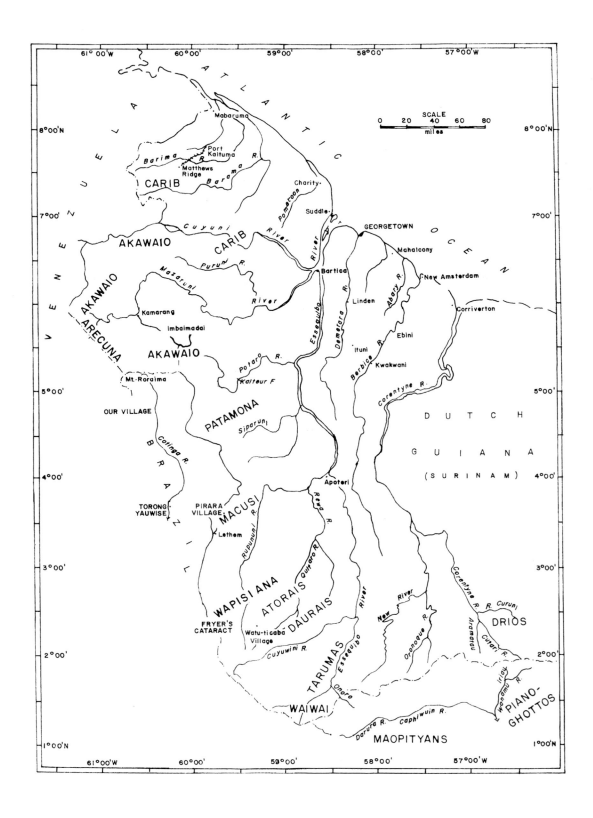

SKETCHES OF
AMERINDIAN TRIBES

GOODALL'S APPOINTMENT AS ARTIST OF
THE SCHOMBURGK EXPEDITION

THE NAME of Robert Schomburgk, the famous explorer-scientist, has eclipsed that of the artist attached to his 1841-43 expedition. The reports and journals of Schomburgk are indeed well known to any scholar of Guyanese history, particularly to those interested in the past Guyana-Venezuela boundary dispute. Reams of paper and armies of words discuss the Schomburgk line, a veritable bone of contention in the nineteenth century. But tucked away in Schomburgk's reports and mentioned a number of times in the work of his brother, Richard, *Travels in British Guiana, 1840-1844*, is a part of the story of the young and promising artist who was asked to share in one of the most arduous and dangerous expeditions undertaken by Robert Schomburgk. This young artist was Edward A. Goodall, the son of a famous engraver, Edward Goodall, and brother of the distinguished London artist, Frederick Goodall. His talent for producing fine water-colours was recognized when at seventeen he won a silver medal from the Society of Arts, London, for a water-colour painting. At the age of twenty-two, he had the unique opportunity of becoming involved in the Schomburgk boundary expedition commissioned by the British government, because of one of those unexpected and unprecedented quirks of history.

Through the auspices of Alexander von Humboldt who had been fascinated by the lush vegetation of the South American continent, Richard Schomburgk, a proficient botanist, was commissioned by the Prussian government to accompany his brother and to collect specimens of the flora and fauna of the Guyana forests for the Royal Museum and the Botanical Gardens in Berlin. Not long after he arrived in British Guiana in 1840 he contracted yellow fever, then a mild epidemic in the colony. It was a fatal disease but miraculously, through the excellent

Map of Guyana showing locations of the major tribes sketched by Goodall and areas reached by the Schomburgk expeditions.

medical attention of Dr Koch of Nurnberg, Schomburgk survived. But fear of succumbing to the dread disease sent Mr W. L. Walton, the commissioned artist of the expedition, scurrying back to England. Another draughtsman had to be found and Goodall was recommended by Colonel Jackson, Secretary of the Royal Geographical Society. It would seem from Colonel Jackson's recommendation that he knew Goodall personally and felt that he was capable of serving as 'photographer' on the Guiana expedition. The Secretary of State, Lord Russell, did not, for he appointed him on the grounds of 'the eminence of the Sponsor' (C.O. 111/184. Colonel Jackson to James Stephen, 29 June 1841). He was granted a salary of £150 per annum as long as the mission continued, as well as an allowance for the payment of his passage to Guiana. Edward Goodall was to live up to the trust which Colonel Jackson placed in him. At the end of the expedition Governor Henry Light wrote to Lord Stanley:

> His [Goodall's] portraits of the various Indian tribes, his drawings of fish and unknown flowers will be a valuable addition to the information already obtained of the natural history of the Interior of British Guiana, and the untutored race now fast disappearing from the earth, who inhabit the wilds.
>
> (C.O. 111/203. Light to Stanley, 14 October 1843)

Goodall was hailed by the local press as 'a talented artist' (*The Royal Gazette*, 19 October 1843). Not long after Schomburgk returned to London, despite his involvement in boundary affairs, he enthusiastically supported Goodall's work, asking the Colonial Office to finance the publication of a work on the Indians sketched by Goodall. He himself would (and who else was more capable?) write the commentaries on the characteristics of the various Indian tribes. The estimated cost of such a publication was £500 but unfortunately art and ethnology had to bow to economics. Though Lord Stanley heartily approved of the project and recommended it to the Lords Commissioners of the Treasury, it was turned down (C.O. 112/28. J. Hope to C. E. Trevelyan, 14 August 1845). From the correspondence between Mr B. Hawes, Under-Secretary of State, and Schomburgk it was clear that Schomburgk still entertained hopes of publishing the sketches (C.O. 112/28. B. Hawes to Schomburgk, 29 April 1847).

Schomburgk had Goodall's botanical sketches displayed in Berlin and the Amerindian sketches in London and Paris. The sketches aroused much interest in the aboriginal inhabitants and their claim for protection which had been emphasized by Schomburgk's journals and supported whole-heartedly by Henry Taylor of the West India Office. They were returned to Goodall who, it seems, must have donated them to the Colonial Office. When next they were heard of, the sketches were in the British Museum. A letter of appreciation from the Secretary of the British Museum read: 'The drawings thus added to the Museum form a collection of great interest and value' (C.O. 111/247. J. Forshall to B. Hawes, 12 May 1847).

What then happened to the artist himself? The hazards of the expeditions in the interior of Guiana must have whetted his appetite for action and danger. In 1854 he left for the Crimea as artist correspondent for the *Illustrated London News*, sending back sixty-five water-colours from the scene of action. He later travelled extensively in Morocco, Spain, Portugal, and Italy. Member of the Royal Water-Colour Society, his paintings won him innumerable prizes and fame. His oil painting of a Guiana subject had attracted the attention of the celebrated water-colourist, J. M. W. Turner, who had it hung in the Royal Academy. But Goodall's fame rests on his water-colours, some of which hang in the museums of London, Liverpool, and Sydney, Australia. As late as 1969 a water-colour 'view of Venice' was sold at Sotheby's for £110. The Amerindian sketches in this volume are no less valuable.

It was this background history of these sketches which aroused my interest in them. The four folios of Goodall's work, fruits of the Schomburgk expedition, were located among the Additional Manuscripts in the British Library, where they had been locked away for over a century. The four volumes contained not only portraits of the various Indian tribes, but also sketches of the occupations of the Indians, landscapes of villages and settlements, river scenes, Indian huts, and the drawings of trees and other flora. In the fourth folio are included the only three drawings (of Demerara) made by that frightened artist, Goodall's predecessor, W. L. Walton. With the exception of the sketches of the flora, the seventy sketches (reduced in size) in this present volume form a representative selection from the four folios in the British Library.

THE 1841–43 EXPEDITIONS

As Everard im Thurn observed: 'Perhaps the most interesting people in British Guiana are the Indians . . .' (*Demerara Papers*, 'Indian Tribes of British Guiana', 1878-79). Every early traveller through the Guiana territory would have heartily endorsed such a view. During his years of travel throughout Guiana, Robert Schomburgk came to understand and appreciate the Indians with whom he had daily contact and on whom he had to depend as guides through the forest region. It was primarily due to his constant pleas that the boundary be defined 'for the benefit of the Indians' that Governor Light and the Colonial Office were made aware that the Indian cause concerned 'British honour and humanity'. Henry Taylor minuted one of Schomburgk's surveys: 'The only questions which seem to make the determination of the boundary a matter of present importance are those connected with the protection of the Indians' (C.O. 111/195. Henry Taylor's Minute in Light to Stanley, 30 October 1842).

Schomburgk's writings underlined his constant concern over the fast decreasing tribes in the interior of British Guiana. The causes he attributed to 'diseases and vices introduced by the settlers, and feuds among themselves'. His conclusion was the one supported by all those who had given evidence before the Committee of the Aboriginal Protection Society, 1836, 'that wherever Europeans have settled, the extermination of the native tribes has succeeded their arrival' (SRo, *Des.*, pp. 48-49). At the end of his first expeditions he estimated the number of Indians to be 7000, pointing out that the Caribs and Atorais were 'fast approaching their extinction' (*Ibid.*, pp. 50–51). This concern of Schomburgk over the decrease of the Indians made him all the more eager to have an 'artist-photographer' capture their likeness. One of Schomburgk's many letters to Governor Light written during the 1841-43 expedition articulated this concern: '. . . . the sketches of Mr Goodall will prove of uncommon interest, as they contain portraits of Indians who have not been hitherto visited by Europeans, and other tribes who are near their extinction' (C.O. 111/204. Schomburgk to Light, 13 October 1843). In a paper read before the Royal Geographical Society on his return from the boundary expedition, Schomburgk listed thirteen tribes: Arawaks, Warraus, Caribs, Accawais, Macusis, Arecunas, Wapisianas, Atorais or Atorias, Tarumas, Woyavais (Wai-Wais), Maopityans, Pianoghottos, and Drios. He stressed that since 1840 smallpox had wiped out large numbers of the Amerindian population (SRo, 'On the Natives of Guiana', 27 November 1844, p. 264). Most of the tribes listed by Schomburgk hold a place in the Goodall 'gallery' of Indians.

The history of these sketches must necessarily be set against the background of the 1841-43 expeditions. As Schomburgk himself tells us 'the pursuit of science alone led him to Guiana'. The writings of Alexander von Humboldt who had travelled in South America during the early part of the nineteenth century but had not penetrated east of the continent, and those of William Hilhouse, a surveyor and correspondent to the Royal Geographical Society, had acted as stimuli for the first Schomburgk expedition to British Guiana in September 1835.

The early expeditions were very fruitful: Schomburgk discovered the water lily named in the Queen's and his honour the *Victoria Regia Schom.* which he considered 'the most beautiful specimen of the Flora of the Western hemisphere'; the tracing of the Essequibo River to its source and the discovery of Roraima were two other notable achievements. He was also given credit for the founding of the Pirara mission on Lake Ammacu in the Rupununi on the Brazilian frontier, an outpost which soon created tension between the Brazilian and British authorities. Above all, his writings were filled with descriptions of the Indians, their customs, culture, and characteristics. Undoubtedly, these 'poor neglected races' intrigued Schomburgk and he pleaded for their civilization, constantly reminding the Home government that it owed a heavy debt to the Indians whose lands Europeans had taken over and whose morals they had corrupted.

His extensive travels throughout the interior of British Guiana and his writings, not only on the Indians but on the resources and potentialities of the 'rich and beautiful country', made him the obvious choice to lead a boundary expedition. In 1840 he was commissioned by the British government to survey and determine the boundaries of the colony. To both his younger brother, Richard, and himself, history, geography, science, and ethnology owe a great deal. The name of Schomburgk remains forever linked with the history of Guyana. As they penetrated into the interior, Richard became even more enraptured by the Indians than by their forest home. Most of the commentaries on the Indians in this book are drawn from his work, which is also filled with geological and botanical information on the riches of the interior of Guyana.

After Walton had hurriedly returned to England, William Leary Echlin, a doctor with some artistic ability, was recruited until another artist could arrive. Echlin, on the first expedition, served more as a doctor than an artist, although he did make a few sketches for Schomburgk. The newly commissioned artist, Edward A. Goodall arrived in Georgetown on Wednesday, 28 July 1841, reported his arrival to Governor Light and on Friday met the Schomburgk brothers. His first impression of 'the Great Traveller' as he labelled Schomburgk was of a 'very nice little man but rather petulant' (GGD). With unusual perception he observed that Schomburgk's present affability and kindness might wear thin once the expedition got under way. Throughout his diary of 23 December 1841-13 June 1842 Goodall was to record Schomburgk's 'damnable bad temper'. At times Goodall's relationship with 'the little man' became extremely stormy. Schomburgk had a terrible temper indeed, quite sensitive to his authority as leader of the expedition, hard on himself and expecting everyone else to 'toe the line'. Nevertheless, as leader of the expedition, he had an overwhelming responsibility to procure Indian guides, to see that the supply of rations was constantly maintained, to map out the trails, and, above all, to safeguard the members of the expedition; he could be excused a few temper tantrums.

Despite the personality clash between the traveller and the artist, Schomburgk was quite pleased with Goodall's artistic ability of which he was assured even before the party left Georgetown. Goodall spent his five months in the capital city making a large number of sketches, most of which were sold. He sketched almost everything—the backdam, ships, horses, flowers, ladies, trees, estates, maps for Schomburgk, and the Public Building for Governor Light. Most of these months, however, were spent working on his famous Georgetown sketches—three panoramic views of Georgetown which he called his Lighthouse sketches because they were sketched from the Lighthouse. Dr Koch, who had nursed Richard Schomburgk so successfully through his bout of yellow fever, shared with Goodall the cost of lithographing and selling the sketches. Many of the families of Georgetown society of the 1840s were collectors of art. Mr H. Dalton, the Deputy Postmaster, afterwards Postmaster of Guiana, was a connoisseur of art, having a collection of portraits himself. Goodall was drawn to the Dalton family not only for art's but for beauty's sake. One of the greatest fascinations Georgetown held for Goodall was pretty Miss Dalton, Mr Dalton's sister. He confessed: 'She is one of the most delightful young ladies I ever saw, and . . . very accomplished, and, without doubt, a remarkably clever girl'. (GGD) Goodall's eye for beauty was not only for the fair sex but also for his surroundings. His pen sketch of a sunrise in Georgetown captured all the delicate lights and shadows of his water-colours:

> It was morning and the rising sun was magnificent. Turner himself, in his most successful bits never approached anything like it for beauty of colour or such magnificence of form. The town was a beautiful clear grey with bright lights shining through the streets leading down to the water's edge and, moor'd along the wharfs in bright relief, white ships and boats with figures of all shades from black to white. (GGD)

His water-colours of various scenes in Georgetown were so well done that Mr Echlin, ex-artist of the earlier expedition, claimed that Goodall could get as much as ten Joes each (£15-£18) for his sketches which, at that time, was quite a large amount for a water-colour sketch. Goodall was somewhat concerned over Schomburgk's enthusiasm for his paintings as he wanted to claim all Goodall's sketches for 'the Guiana expedition'. Goodall feared that he would not 'have a single sketch' to call his own.

After his first frustrating experience with bureaucratic red tape (he had difficulty in getting his passage money when he arrived), Goodall became involved in the social life of 'the genteel and lovely world of Georgetown', a world where, according to Richard Schomburgk, pleasure was the hallmark of the society among both the upper and lower classes. Young Goodall enjoyed all Georgetown had to offer—he dined at the Governor's and with a number of families, fenced, played chess, listened to music, went shooting, riding, dancing, attended the races and church, visited neighbouring estates, and read avidly during the long, rainy days. His diary paints a picture of a very athletic and energetic young man, cultured and talented. The combination of high spirits and talent were both necessary for the job ahead of him.

THE EXPEDITIONS INTO THE INTERIOR
OF THE GUIANA FORESTS

The party, consisting of the Schomburgk brothers, Mr W. J. Fryer as Schomburgk's secretary, Goodall, and a few aides left Georgetown on the morning of 23 December 1841. It must have been difficult to leave the Garden City with its gracious living and enter a world of fast-flowing rivers and dense forests where survival was a daily occupation. Christmas was spent at Ampa Station and a few days later the expedition left for Pirara, stopping at Bartica Grove to pick up the Reverend Thomas Youd. On the opening days of the journey up the Essequibo River, Goodall began his first sketches. At Waraputa, the mission established by the Revd Youd after his expulsion from Pirara by the Brazilians, Goodall sketched the village despite the continuous rainfall. Goodall also mentioned his sketching the Waraputa Falls but made no comment on the famous Amerindian hieroglyphics engraved on the rocks there. (These are fully described with illustrations in Richard Schomburgk's work.) Before the party reached Pirara Goodall bore the brunt of Schomburgk's bad temper after scaring him by setting fire to a huge Mora tree. His punishment was to make two sketches—not an easy task, commented Goodall, 'after sitting in a corial all day' (GED). Schomburgk had no patience with what he probably considered a schoolboy prank which could well have had disastrous consequences.

After six weeks travelling by corial along the rapids of the Essequibo River the outskirts of Pirara were reached. The detachment of British troops despatched to protect both the Indians and the land from Brazilian aggression arrived soon after, swearing that Pirara 'must be the last place God Almighty made' (GED). The British flag was raised at Pirara and Schomburgk became very involved in diplomatic affairs. He had already informed the Brazilians of the arrival of the boundary expedition and of the coming of Her Majesty's Forces. At a subsequent conference held with Captain Antonio Leal, Commandant of Fort San Joaquin and Fray José, Lieutenant E. H. Bingham in command of the British troops, Captain Bush, his adjutant, and Schomburgk, all agreed to an amicable compromise and to refrain from using force. According to Goodall the meeting seemed rather convivial, despite the tense circumstances. Nevertheless, after Schomburgk later claimed for Her Majesty's Government the right bank of the Takutu as the south-western boundary of British Guiana with its navigation and fishing rights, the Brazilians immediately lodged an official protest.

With the exception of the brief excitement of the *pourparlers* between the British and Brazilian military officials, life in Pirara was boring. It was, therefore, not surprising that tempers were short. Schomburgk berated Goodall, unfortunately in front of the officers, for leaving the village without his permission. Ruffled tempers were soothed after a while but flared up again on the march. Walking under a burning tropical sun, wading through marshes, and lashed by torrential rainstorms which threatened to destroy food supplies, did little to restore Schomburgk's temper. Within three months of the expedition leaving Georgetown, Goodall was both 'exasperated with the damned insects' and 'thoroughly disgusted' with Schomburgk (GED). He continued his work, however, making sketches of Pirara and the Indians. Schomburgk's admiration for the artist's work in no way neutralized his impatience with the young man who quite obviously baulked against his martinet control of the expedition. The journey up the Takutu was an exacting one—lengthy, fatiguing marches, the exhausting cutting of trails through the bush, and, above all, the scarcity of water pushed the party to the limits of endurance. The Cotinga-Roraima expedition brought new experiences. While Schomburgk exulted over 'the botanical El Dorado' (SRi, II, 218) and his brother, Richard collected hundreds of species of plants from 'the inexhaustible . . . treasure-house', Goodall was unable to sketch Roraima as his fingers were stiff from the cold and the paper wet with the damp. The dangerous rapids which the party encountered were both a challenge and a threat. Goodall almost lost his life when the expedition shot the Aratiari Rapids (SRi, II, 233), and again en route to Watu-Ticaba. Mr Fryer and himself were saved by three Indians when the canoe was whirled around in the current. The cataract was called Fryer's Cataract; one is left to wonder why not after Goodall as well whose life had also been in jeopardy there (SRi, II, 298). Later maps show Goodall's Cataract on the Corentyne River not far from its junction with the New River, but there is no reference in the writings of either Schomburgk to the occasion when this cataract received its name. The narrow escape with his life might have helped to improve the Schomburgk-Goodall relationship. After the Cotinga-Roraima expedition, in forwarding Goodall's sketches to Governor Light, Schomburgk specifically commented on Goodall's industry and 'his amiable conduct' (Schomburgk's Report, 23 January 1843). While enjoining his brother and Mr Fryer to conduct the baggage and instruments safely back to Georgetown, Schomburgk took Goodall on his last expedition 'To explore the regions from the sources of the Essequibo to the sources of the Corentyn' (Schomburgk's Report, 25 August 1842). He claimed that Goodall was needed 'to depict some of these Indian tribes which are scarcely known by name in the colony, much less in Europe' (Schomburgk's Report, 18 May 1843).

It is unfortunate that Goodall's diary ends in June 1842 and his views of the Cotinga-Roraima expedition and, above all, the Corentyne do not enhance Schomburgk's factual reports as well as add another dimension to Richard Schomburgk's work. Undoubtedly, the expedition which left Watu-Ticaba on 3 June 1843 and arrived in Georgetown almost four months later was a thrilling, hazardous, and unforgettable one. The party set out to explore an uncharted and unknown terrain, among strange tribes. Richard Schomburgk underlined that fact when they parted at Watu-Ticaba; it might well have been a last good-bye (SRi, II, 312).

The unpredictable behaviour of the Maopityan guides, the suspicions of the Pianoghottos, the dwindling of the food supplies, the hazards of traversing the turbulent falls in frail wood-skins, the laborious and constant portaging, all added up to the most difficult journey of the whole survey expedition. Schomburgk and Goodall were the only Europeans on this expedition. Utterly exhausted in body paddling for days without rest, but exulting in spirit, they reached Berbice on 9 October 1843. The mammoth task of the boundary survey was accomplished in less than the estimated time and without loss of life. Indeed, the Prussian Columbus had every right to be enormously gratified as he had traversed 'thousands of miles never before trodden by the foot of civilised man . . . many not even by the savage Indian' (Schomburgk's Report, 13 October 1843). Goodall shared in this glory. While Schomburgk's fame rested on his achievement of surveying a vast tropical territory, on his valuable maps, and on the priceless collection of the flora and fauna of Guiana, Goodall's revolved around his capturing for posterity in his realistic illustrations, the Indian tribes, their occupations, and their environment. Nevertheless, it was Robert Schomburgk who occupied the limelight and not long after his return from Guiana, he was knighted by the Queen, an honour he well deserved. But not even as Sir Robert could he cajole economic support from the Treasury for the publication of the Goodall sketches. Now, more than 125 years later the sketches have come into their own.

INDIAN MIGRATIONS INTO GUIANA AND
INDIAN CHARACTERISTICS

The value of the Goodall sketches lies most of all in the wealth of anthropological and ethnological knowledge they offer on the aboriginal tribes of the country, especially those who are now extinct in Guyana: the Maiongkongs, the Maopityans, the Drios, Tarumas, Amaripas, and Pianoghottos. Most of the well-known history of the Indians is that recorded of the Caribs, Arawaks, Warraus, and Akawaio. Not surprisingly, reports of early travellers vary regarding the names and numbers of the tribes they met or heard of in the Guiana territory. It is well documented that the Dutch were closely allied with the Caribs and the Arawaks to whom they gave presents for their services in capturing runaway slaves, in reporting Spanish movements in the north-west and west of the territory, and most important, in giving valuable assistance during the slave revolts. More detailed observations on the Indians date from the British period after 1803. William Hilhouse, an ex-Quartermaster-General of Indians, 1823, who lived among the Indians and was himself married to an Indian, wrote that six Indian tribes lived in the territory: the Caribs, Akawaio, Arawak, Warrau, Macusi, and Paramona (Patamona) (H, 'Book of Reconnaissances . . .'). A few years later he added the Attaraya (Atorai), and the Attamacka to the list (H, *Indian Notices*, p. 7). Schomburgk's number varied between 1837-43 from eight to thirteen, understandably so, as by 1843 he had covered most of the Guiana territory and encountered the hardly known tribes in the south and south-east, the Maiongkongs, Maopityans, Tarumas, Pianoghottos, and Drios whom Goodall portrayed. There were very few people who had any first hand knowledge of the Indians. The Revd W. H. Brett of the Society for the Propagation of the Gospel spent forty years as a missionary to the Indians. He wrote comprehensively on the Indians, and told of far distant ones, the 300 Zaparas, offspring of the Macusis and Arecunas, and the Zamaratas, a tribe closely resembling the Drios (BIM, pp. 298, 300). From the reports of W. C. F. McClintock, Postholder and Superintendent of Rivers and Creeks on the Pomeroon for thirty-three years, a vast amount of information about the customs and characteristics of the Indians was obtained. Knowledgeable though these few were regarding the culture of the Indians, it was generally admitted that 'To trace the early history of the aboriginal tribes was a task of great difficulty' (BIM, p. 274). Brett deduced that the Macusi was the tribe whom Sir Walter Ralegh met on the Orinoco in 1595 and who were later pushed northwards by the Wapisiana; the Arawaks, mild and peaceable, were harried from the islands, the Bahamas, Cuba, Haiti, Jamaica, and Puerto Rico by the bellicose Caribs who were themselves later expelled by the Europeans, returning to the mainland from where, according to Brett, they imagined they had come (BIM, pp. 278-83). The Arawaks were found by Columbus and Ralegh on the mouth of the Orinoco, probably moving eastwards into Guiana territory to escape the Spaniards (*Ibid.*, pp. 283-89). Hilhouse and the Schomburgks merely noted their location and estimated their numbers. In 1883 Sir Everard F. im Thurn published his celebrated work, *Among the Indians of Guiana*, the result of his travels in the interior and his complete fascination with the Indian tribes. His was the first serious study of the origin of the tribes and he, too, admitted the impossibility of giving any accurate information on the time and place from whence the so-called aboriginal inhabitants arrived in the territory. He divided the tribes into two categories: (1) native tribes, and (2) stranger tribes, basing his deduction on 'the common feeling of aversion' which the native

THE SKETCHES:
THEIR VALUE AS A VISUAL RECORD
OF TRIBAL LORE

The Warraus, represented by the sixteen-year-old boy (Plate 1), were acclaimed by all who met them as *the* canoe builders of the coastlands; they also had the rather unsavoury reputation of being the dirtiest of all the tribes, possibly because they lived in the swamps and marshes. Although J. J. Hartsinck described them as lazy, McClintock praised them as 'the most useful of all the Indians that British Guiana can boast of . . .' (McClintock's Report, 26 February 1849).

Three sketches depict a man and woman of the Carib tribe (Plates 2, 3, 4). The Carib village at Waraputa on the Essequibo River was ruled over by the Carib chief, Irai-i, grandson of the notorious Mahanavra, who had once strutted into Georgetown demanding presents from Governor H. L. Carmichael. Irai-i proudly wore the gold crescent medallion-sign of Carib sovereignty (SRi, II, 247), but it was Francisco, wearing a European shirt whom Goodall painted. Francisco was a convert to Christianity, and European clothing more than anything else was a symbol of such conversion, (Governor Henry Light always reasoned rather naively that a clothed Indian was a Christian Indian). The expedition came across another Carib settlement of five houses on the southern bank of the Rupununi, one of the main tributaries of the Essequibo. Here the 'irresistible master-key'—liquor—metamorphosed a surly chieftain into a most friendly and obliging fellow (SRi, I, 68).

Though the captions of the paintings call these Indians Caribisi, im Thurn's writings explained that the word 'Caribisi' was not the correct name for that tribe. It was used by the Arawaks to indicate Carib settlements—Caribisi, that is, 'Caribs live there' but travellers erroneously deduced that it was the name of the tribe (imT, p. 164). im Thurn was the first to differentiate between the Carib branch and the tribes of the True Carib, Akawoi (Akawaoi), Macusi, and Arecuna who belong to that branch. In Plate 3 one of the Carib women is spinning cotton—an almost daily chore among Indian women who both gather and spin the cotton particularly for the making of hammocks. Cotton is especially used by the Caribs. It is claimed that the Caribs brought with them the skill of using the spindle. The other tribes who used to spin cotton on their thighs adopted the spindle method, this fact lending support to the late migration theory of the Caribs into Guiana (imT, pp.287-88). Indian women are hard workers; they plant and reap the cassava, continuously make cassava bread and piwari drink, a fermented beverage concocted from burnt cassava bread, gather firewood, cook, manufacture hammocks, apron belts, baskets and pottery, and carry the baggage on trips, all while raising a family. Yet there is a division of labour which upholds the dominance of the men; they build the houses and canoes, shape the bows and arrows, and blow guns, go hunting and fishing, and competently lead the way on expeditions into the bush.

Near the Rewa, another large tributary of the Rupununi, a busy settlement of the Macusis astonished the members of the expedition with its hustle and bustle. Richard Schomburgk eloquently described the Macusi as one of 'the most beautiful tribes of Guiana' (SRi, I, 280). Goodall obviously held the same view, judging by his twenty-four sketches of these people. As the party made Pirara its headquarters for subsequent expeditions many months were spent in Macusi territory. Each tribe is unique in some way; the Macusis of the Carib branch but darker than the True Caribs hold the palm as the concoctors and users of the famous ourali poison (*Strychnos toxifera*) more commonly known as curare, and sometimes written as worali or urali. It is a deadly poison with which they tip their arrows, shooting them from blowpipes. For their skill in the preparation of the ourali poison they are much feared by the Caribs and Akawois, and probably because of this gained the reputation of being 'cruel and revengeful' (H. 'Book of Reconnaissances . . .', p.27). On the other hand, Richard Schomburgk with months of experience to judge them, praised them as 'peace-loving, complaisant, gentle and friendly' (SRi, II, 246). Brett described them as 'industrious and unwarlike' people, a fact which laid them open to attack by other tribes (BIM, p. 276).

The customs and characteristics of the Macusis are fully described in Volume II of Richard Schomburgk's *Travels in British Guiana, 1840-1844*. The Macusis were rarely polygamous, had strict marriage tests for prospective husbands, made loving marriage partners and doting parents, and practised *couvade* (on the birth of a child the father lay in his hammock and received the congratulations of his friends while the mother went busily about her household chores with suckling child). Their belief in a spirit world was strong—Makonaima, the one who worked by night, was worshipped as a Supreme Being. The chief held authority over the settlement, an authority that was hardly exercised in peace since members of the tribe carried out their particular role in the society. Justice was meted out in the spirit of the 'lex talionis'.

Both Macusi men and women love adornment. Plates 16, 18, 19, and 20 illustrate this propensity. Feathers and beads, pierced noses and lips, and a string of teeth for a necklace mark the ornament of the men who, it is contended, in all primitive societies are more gorgeously decorated than the women. Of the two main ornaments worn by men, the necklace of teeth, usually of animals which the Indian himself has killed, is the more prized possession because it denotes the owner's skill as a hunter. The Macusi women are particularly fascinated by beads with which they love to deck themselves and for which they are willing to barter their huts if possible! The weapon of the Macusi, the blowpipe, is especially noted (Plates 20, 22). It is peculiar to the savannah tribes and, of course, common among many other South American tribes. im Thurn described blowpipes very simply as 'tubes of very great length, often from 12 to 16 feet or more, through which a small dart is blown' (imT, p.246). The dart, about five or six inches long, is tipped with the ourali poison. Where the explosion of a gun frightens away birds and animals, the noiseless blowpipe effectively drops its prey at a range of forty to fifty feet.

On the outskirts of Pirara the Revd Thomas Youd (whom the Revd J. Bernau claimed had died on his way back to England from the effects of the ourali poison) introduced the Schomburgks and Goodall to Basiko, the old one-eyed Macusi chief who seemed genuinely delighted to see Youd again. Goodall painted Basiko playing a reed instrument (Plate 11). In plates 6 and 15 Macusi girls are depicted playing bamboo flutes, the Quana and Kaikara respectively. These reed instruments are particularly manufactured by the savannah Indians.

An interesting Macusi was Aiyukante (Plate 14), a piaiman (shaman or medicine man), who accompanied the party on the Takutu expedition with his bride-to-be, Baru, of whom he was intensely jealous. He probably had good cause for this jealousy as Richard Schomburgk called her 'the prettiest Macusi girl in Pirara' (SRi, II, 111). Could she be the Paro (Plate 13) painted by Goodall? Schomburgk does not enlighten us on that point. Baru, however, disliked her fiancé and begged protection from him from Youd and the Schomburgks. It was a delicate situation, as according to Indian customary 'law' Baru already belonged to Aiyukante. Robert Schomburgk sent Aiyukante away on the pretext of procuring more men for the projected expedition to Roaima, then hustled Baru back to Pirara. On his return Aiyukante furiously demanded Baru but was threatened on pain of death to follow her. Surprisingly he accepted the situation and stayed with the expedition (SRi, II, 112). At Nappi, Richard Schomburgk praised one of the guides 'Good old Pureka' for looking after him during his attacks of fever. Plate 15 shows Purreka, a Macusi girl from Nappi. One would like to think that Purreka was the young wife of Pureka whom Goodall painted in gratitude. On very few occasions did either Richard Schomburgk or Goodall specifically mention the names of the Indians who were being painted; one can only speculate as to the identities of the models.

In Plates 10, 20, 21, 22, and 23 Goodall portrayed all the details of the Macusi dwellings. In Plate 10 two types of dwellings are shown: the beehive, bell tent or circular house peculiar to the Macusis, Wapisianas, and Arecunas, and somewhat similar to those of the Maopityans (Plates 60 and 61); and the second a square shed where the Macusis relax in their hammocks during the day. Along the cross-beams are bows and arrows, ornaments and gourds, while in the left-hand corner is the usual boat-shaped trough for piwari. Cooking utensils and gourds lie strewn on the ground. On the roof of the beehive house is another typical feature of life in every Amerindian settlement, whether it be in the forest or savannah: large, round discs of freshly made cassava bread dry out to a crispness. It should be noted that the roof and walls of the beehive houses are very substantially made and plastered with mud to keep out the cold night winds that blow through the savannahs. The tall forest trees delicately painted by the artist provide a fitting background to these huts.

While the party was still at Pirara, some Maiongkongs arrived from the Cunucununi River on the upper Orinoco en route to Georgetown to barter their hammocks, graters and hunting dogs for axes—a journey of over 1000 miles in three months! Robert Schomburgk, who had met the Maiongkongs on his 1837 expedition and had described them as tall and muscular, a haughty people, skilled in boat-building (SRo, *Travels* . . . , pp. 16, 68), delightedly renewed old acquaintances. Fortunately for the Maiongkongs, Schomburgk's party was able to supply the axes, and with no cause, therefore, to go any further they spent a few days in Pirara. This gave Goodall time enough to sketch one of them with his famous hunting dogs (Plate 24). Very little is known of the Maiongkongs who came from across the Venezuelan border. In his diary, Goodall called them the 'Mionkougs' (or is it a slip in the transcription?), and observed that Schomburgk had to cajole one to sit for him. It was always difficult to get the Indians to sit willingly for their portraits. Seeing their likeness suddenly appear under the skilful fingers of Goodall, their superstitious minds probably connected the whole business with magic. Thus the innumerable sketches produced by Goodall testify, above all, to his patience and perserverance with his somewhat unwilling models.

On the Cotinga-Roraima expedition, an extremely difficult one through savannahs and swamps, dense vegetation and rushing cataracts, Goodall, as well as Richard Schomburgk, succumbed to bouts of fever. Thus there was little time and less energy for sketching. There was a pleasant interlude at the Macusi village of Torong-Yauwise (Plate 68) where in full ceremonial dress of feathers and paint, war-clubs, bows and arrows, the Macusis, Wapisianas, and Arecunas turned out, beating drums and blowing flutes to greet the Paranaghieris or strangers. Richard Schomburgk said that the six white men among the 400 Indians of different tribes felt perfectly safe and happy, enjoying the entertainment of song and dance to which they were treated (SRi, II, 151).

This expedition carried the travellers into Arecuna country. They were warmly received at Yawangra where, however, through the scarcity of provisions, the Arecunas could offer them no more than friendliness (SRi, II, 163-64). The Arecunas inhabited the mountain areas and savannahs near the sources of the Caroni, Cuyuni, and Mazaruni, closer to the Venezuelan border. In 1837 and 1841 Schomburgk estimated the number of those in the British territory at 500 (SRo, *Des . . .* , p. 50 and SRi, II, 163). In the valley of the Kukenam the Arecuna chief gave them a royal welcome, not only in his lengthy speech but in the greetings of the women and children. The chief's wife and daughter personally served the hungry travellers with all they possessed, an illustration of that most excellent trait of the Amerindian—his hospitality. The men wore bamboo sticks in their noses, lips and ears, as can be seen in Plates 26 and 27.

Because of the friendly reception given them in that area the travellers built their 'village' of six houses there among the Arecunas. They were lost in admiration at the 'fantastic feather-crowns' of the men (Plate 27) but young Goodall was swept off his feet by a dark-eyed, ebony-haired beauty—'the most perfect female figure that we had ever seen amongst the Indians', as Richard Schomburgk described her (SRi, II, 188). So infatuated was Goodall by this beauty, Cummiyaure, that, instead of painting her, 'the passionate artist' rashly asked her father if he could marry her! The following morning the wise father lost no time in removing Cummiyaure, who was obviously enjoying the situation, from temptation. Unfortunately, Goodall lost the opportunity of immortalizing in paint this Helen of the Arecunas. But he did paint a young Arecuna (Plate 28), Tamanua, 'a most beautiful boy' (SRi, II, 190), who so charmed all the travellers with his gracious ways that Robert Schomburgk wanted to take him to Georgetown. Another wise father, a tall, outstanding Arecuna with his macaw feather-crown, hurriedly took him away from the village.

In an earlier expedition from Pirara to the source of the Tacutu the travellers arrived at a Wapisiana settlement at Tenette. Because of its lush forest vegetation this area held great interest for Richard, the botanist. But even more interesting than the environment were the people—the Wapisianas—great hunters and avid smokers, tall and well-built; the women with beautiful, black, shiny hair which fell in cascades to their calves. But the women were as shy as they were beautiful, and Goodall, who could hardly wait to sketch them, had a difficult time in persuading them to model (SRi, II, 32).

According to im Thurn, the Wapisianas together with the Arawaks, Warraus, and Caribs constitute one of the main branch tribes and could also be considered one of the native tribes (imT, pp.163, 171). In 1837 Robert Schomburgk gave their number as 500, Brett in 1851 as 400. They were the traders of the area, the 'middlemen' between the Tarumas and the Macusis; as 'the great canoe-makers of the interior', they bartered them, together with hammocks obtained from the Macusis, for the cassava graters and hunting dogs of the Tarumas. The Macusis traded their ourali poison and cotton hammocks for the graters and the dogs (imT, pp. 169, 273).

It was at Watu-Ticaba, the jumping off point for the last journey of the expedition—the Corentyne safari—that Goodall did most of his sketches of the Wapisianas. The chieftain of Watu-Ticaba, Wayapari, was even more impressive and picturesque than the settlement with its five large beehive houses and its fifty-eight inhabitants. He was what one would call an unforgettable character. Goodall faithfully captured the likeness of this friendly old chief (Plate 31) who obviously considered himself up-to-date on protocol by greeting the European travellers in a rather bizarre 'State dress' of sailor's trousers, a dagger stuck through a blue loin cloth, a red woollen cap with tassels, the ensemble finished off with a blue umbrella—his most prized possession. Whenever it rained, Wayapari took great pains to remove his only wardrobe, wrap the umbrella and dagger in the clothes and revert to the natural (SRi, II, 303). Among the interesting people met at Watu-Ticaba was a Negro slave who, forty years before, had escaped from the Rio Negro, lived among the Wapisianas and married into their tribe. Warehre, the son of that union, is depicted in Plates 66 and 67. Though the blend of the Indian and African features can be seen, Plate 66 emphasizes the fact that his culture is Indian—he is in full Indian dress. Most interesting of all is the old Amaripa woman, Miaha, 'the last of her race' (Plate 43), who had no stories to pass on of a race that had already died out. Age and memories of years long past are etched on her face.

On the last stage of the expedition up the Corentyne and its tributaries, Schomburgk and Goodall encountered the Atorai, Daurai, Taruma, Maopityan, Pianoghotto, and Drio tribes. In the virgin forest, not far from Watu-Ticaba the party arrived at the Atorai settlement which consisted of one large round house with six hammocks. A Daurai village on the Guidaru (Quitaro) visited before by Schomburgk when there were forty inhabitants was now a pathetic sight, with only two adults and a few children. The Atorai, a sister tribe of the Wapisiana branch, lived to the south of the Wapisianas. Robert Schomburgk did not meet them on his first expeditionn in the 1830s but had been told of their existence by the Wapisianas; together with the Daurais they were then thought to number 200. im Thurn supposed that the Macusis and the Arecunas had taken over the savannah territory once the domain of the Wapisianas, Atorais, and Amaripas (imT, p.173). He felt that the Atorai, Daurai, and Taurai were identical tribes though to a certain extent he conceded the Schomburgk view that the Atorai differed from the Daurai and Taurai who were identical (imT, p. 158). Writing in the early twentieth century, W. C. Farabee concluded that the Atorai no longer existed as a separate tribe; their language had died out. 'Physically, linguistically and culturally they are closely related to the Wapisianas' by whom they had been absorbed through intermarriage (Farabee, pp. 12, 14, 132). In his article 'Extinct Tribes and Threatened Species of the South Savannahs', N. O. Poonai claims that there are a few survivors of the Atorai at Schiwib (Poonai, p. 80). Plates 37, 38, 39, 40 and 41 capture the features of these almost forgotten people.

Twenty days after leaving Watu-Ticaba Schomburgk, Goodall and their guides arrived at the first Taruma settlement where they were given sugar-cane grown in great quantities by the Tarumas. At the second settlement Schomburgk met an old acquaintance of the 1837 expedition, the Barokoto chief, Yarimoko. They found the Tarumas there in the midst of a piwari feast (Plate 45). Both a corial and a trough contained the piwari, the *sine qua non* of every Amerindian feast. Feasts are held to celebrate birth, marriage, and death; sometimes they are held just for the sake of celebrating. With the trough holding about 150-200 gallons of piwari, getting intoxicated is an integral part of such a feast.

In 1837 Schomburgk described the Taruma tribe as a fine, athletic people numbering about 500. The darkest of all the tribes, the Tarumas were latecomers into the Guiana territory. Near the end of the seventeenth century they were reported as inhabiting the mouth of the Rio Negro in Brazil where the Carmelites had a mission among them. It was alleged that rough treatment by the Portuguese resulted in their migrating north. A map by Juan de la Cruz Cano y Olmedilla, 1771-75, located them in the upper Essequibo region. This led the archaeologists Evans and Meggers to date their migration into Guiana in the eighteenth century (Evans and Meggers, *Archaeological Investigations. . . ,* p. 263). According to accounts by Richard Schomburgk and the Revd Brett it was Mahanarva, 'notorious cacique of the Caribs', who, in 1810, brought word to the government in Georgetown of the existence of this tribe. His story, a rather outlandish one, described the Tarumas as an amphibious people. The body markings on the Taruma woman (Plate 49) illustrate the theory that the deeper in the interior a tribe lives the more do its members paint their bodies. Schomburgk was the first European to visit this tribe and his brother asserted that no other tribe had ever received him 'with such devoted hospitality' (SRi, II,375).

The Tarumas were not too happy about the travellers' journey to the Corentyne or Curitani as they called it. It was only by a clever ruse that Schomburgk was able to persuade Yarimoko to guide them to the Maopityans from whom they hoped to obtain more definite information on the Corentyne route. Schomburgk left these people, saddened at the decrease in their numbers. In six years an estimated 500 people had dwindled to 150. According to Richard Schomburgk their continuous decrease was caused by too much inbreeding which produced few and sickly offspring (SRi, II, 375). von Martius considered the Tarumas extinct by 1867. On the Amazon expedition in 1916, however, Farabee found a few survivors but observed that most of the tribe had been decimated by disease. Evans and Meggers, writing in 1960, claimed that their culture had become extinct by 1925; by 1952 only four adult survivors lived among the Wai-Wai (Evans and Meggers, p. 339).

It was a long, hard trek from the Taruma settlement to the valley of the Darura, a tributary of the Caphiwuin. Here, nestled in the forest were two large beehive houses, the Maopityan settlement (Plates 60, 61). The Wapisianas called this tribe Maopityans, Mao meaning Frog and Pityan, people or tribe. The Maopityans called themselves Mawakwas. Because of a lack of knowledge of their vocabulary im Thurn was unable to classify these people. Farabee stated that they were Mapidians—his theory being that they called themselves Pidians, people, and the Wapisianas added the Ma meaning 'not'(Farabee, p. 158). This tribe, which Schomburgk felt had been 'a once powerful tribe', was now reduced to thirty-nine individuals (SRi, II, 377-78).

Like Schomburgk, Barrington Brown commented on the unusual shape of the head of the Maopityans, long, narrow and high, and claimed that it was artificially formed by applying pieces of wood to the sides of the child's head (B, p.246). Schomburgk, on the other hand, affirmed on his experience of seeing a new-born infant that the Maopityans were born with elongated heads (SRi, II, 377). It is probable that Barrington Brown deduced that the Maopityans had a similar custom to that of the Mayas of the Yucatan who, for beauty's sake, compressed the heads of their children between two boards.

From the number of portraits of these people (reproduced as Plates 51–59) it would seem that Goodall was obviously fascinated by the Maopityans. Plate 58 is a delicate and touching madonna suckling her child. The dancing dress of feathers is elaborately shown in Plate 56.

The Maopityans gave Schomburgk and Goodall directions to the Corentyne—they should travel down the Caphiwuin to the south of the Wanamu where they would encounter the settlements of the Pianoghottos and the Drios. The frightened Maopityans were not inclined to wander too far from their own territory and gave Schomburgk an anxious time by running off into the forest, taking with them the provisions from the expedition. It was almost a month later, after hazardous travelling through dense forest and along treacherous rapids in frail woodskins, before Schomburgk, Goodall and guides met the Pianoghottos. Seeing strangers approaching, the Pianoghottos, panic-stricken, evacuated their settlements. It was only under dire threats that the fugitive Maopityans were constrained to locate the Pianoghottos. Not long after the party crossed the Aramatau River they finally caught up with the vanishing Pianoghottos, who, it seemed, had mistaken the strange men in the woodskins for the Tschikianas, a dreaded neighbour. Plates 62, 63, and 64 illustrate this tribe, seen for the first time by Schomburgk and Goodall. The village of the Pianoghottos on the Cutari, a tributary of the Corentyne, consisted of three houses, one similar to that of the Maopityans, the others two open sheds. These people told Schomburgk not only of the geography of the area but of the other tribes to be found in the surrounding territory: the Orokoyanna or Parrot Indians, the Drios, the Tunayannas or Water Indians, the Maipurischiannas or Tapir Indians, and the Barokotos (SRi, II, 383). Plate 62 shows the Pianoghotto chieftain in rather similar attire to that of the Maopityans.

Apart from including the Pianoghottos in his list of tribes as a sub-tribe of the Caribs and observing that they were an isolated tribe, im Thurn offered no information regarding their customs or characteristics; he had never seen them. In the 1900s a traveller, O. Coudreau, encountered the tribe and devoted a chapter to the Pianocoto (Pianoghottos) in 'Voyage Au Cumina, 20 April 1900-07'. From a brief stay among these people found then on the Paru, a tributary of the Cumina River in Brazil, Coudreau noted that they were hunters and fishers, shooting fish with arrows tipped with curare. He regretted not being able to give more detailed information about the Pianoghottos but, of course, was able to describe them and comment on their occupations: 'They were of medium stature, well proportioned. Their hair is black, greasy and stiff . . . their eyes are slightly oblique . . . the skin is a very light yellow there where the roucou (dye) is rubbed off' (Coudreau, p. 157). Some wore necklaces of beads; none were tattooed but had scars on their arms made with tiger teeth; their ears were pierced. Clothing consisted of laps of loin cloths, and fringed cotton bands around the arms and legs. The division of labour was similar to that among other tribes: while the men hunted and fished, the women spun cotton, made stringed hammocks, bead aprons, laps, cotton bands and some pottery. Coudreau commented at length on the suspicious nature of the Pianoghottos, a trait also noted by Schomburgk, but concluded, after learning of their past experiences with other tribes and the bush negroes, that they had every right to be wary of strangers.

On the Cutari River, the Drios, a fellow tribe of the Pianoghottos, were found. These people tattooed their bodies, unlike the Pianoghottos who painted theirs with the roucou, but they were similar in features and customs. Goodall seemed to have had time to paint only one Drio—a female of the tribe (Plate 65). Barrington Brown, travelling in the same area in 1876, came across the remains of the Drio settlements but saw no signs of any Indians, either Drios or Pianoghottos. According to W. E. Roth, the Trios and Drios are one and the same tribe and could be found on the upper Tapanahoni, a branch of the Maroni River which forms the eastern border of Surinam. They were also known as the Tlio and the Kiliu. In his 'Report of the Tapanahoni Expedition' (translated by W. E. Roth, 1923), A. Franssen Herderschee wrote that the Trios were also called the Akuli-yu and the Akoeri who lived on the Corentyne were enemies of the Caribs. On the assurance of the bush negroes, he claimed that the Akoeris 'were no other than the Trios' (Herderschee, p. 974). Among his observations on the Trios, Herderschee stated that they had the secret of the curare poison, but it seems that unlike the Macusis, they had no blowpipes and merely tipped their arrow points with the curare. Like the Pianoghottos they trained hunting dogs and cultivated cotton. Their villages were to be found on the Paloemeu, a tributary of the Tapanahoni, and the Koereni (Courouni, Curuni), (Herderschee, p.977). In an article written in 1972 on the 'Amerindians of Surinam', Peter Kloos spoke of the Trios on the Courouni, Tapanahoni and Paloemeu Rivers in Surinam and on the East and West Paru and Marapi in Brazil. They had been dying out, but in the 1960s missionary work halted their decline. From the observations of P. G. Riviere who lived among them between 1963-64 and subsequently wrote his work on *Marriage among the Trio: A Principle of Social Organisation* (Oxford, 1969), the Trios numbered 380 concentrated in two villages on the Curuni and Paloemeu. It would, therefore, not be a too far-fetched deduction to conclude that the Trios in Surinam today are the descendants of the Drios of Schomburgk's day. The Curuni, tributary of the Corentyne, runs parallel to the Cutari on which the Drios were found and branches out in the direction of the Tapanahoni. To the Indians political or geographical boundaries posed no problems; they moved freely between territories. Thus, although the Drios no longer live within the Guyana border, they obviously continue to exist in Surinam. So too are the Maopityans and Pianoghottos known to exist in Brazilian territory. The Wai-Wais, of whom im Thurn had once written 'only their name is known' (imT, p.163), are now the only tribe in the far distant south of Guyana.

Richard Schomburgk wrote that 'smallpox was undoubtedly the most devastating and probably also the last scourge to seal the doomed extinction of the Guiana aborigines' (SRi, II, 293). The Revd Brett had reported that between 1841-54 smallpox and measles had wiped out the Indians, followed in 1857 by cholera, and in 1865 by the Carib sickness, an infectious disease (BIT, pp. 223-25). Both Schomburgk and Brett referred to the Arawaks, Warraus, Caribs, Akawois, and Macusis—tribes that had come in contact with European diseases. But what of those tribes that rarely, if ever, saw a white man? Schomburgk's party might have been the first and last group of Euopeans to cross the path of the tribes in the south and south-east within their life-time. Inter-tribal wars had, no doubt, helped to reduce the numbers in each tribe. It has already been noted that one alleged cause of the gradual extinction of the Tarumas was inbreeding. The Atorais, according to the observations of archaeologists, were absorbed into the Wapisiana tribe. But what of the Maopityans, Pianoghottos, and Drios? What had caused the diminution of numbers among these people? Poonai claimed that the latter groups involuntarily entered the Guiana territory to escape oppression. Faced with 'a hostile environment' and already broken in mind and body, they 'lost the will to survive' (Poonai, p. 79). Yet, it can be argued, in a period when boundaries were not defined, how did the Indians know in whose territory they were living? The Maopityans and Pianoghottos merely moved south and south-east into a less hostile environment, the Drios west. The Toynbee view of the loss of nerve would be a more convincing one if we had some accurate knowledge of the numbers of the tribes that came from the south and east and an approximate period of their arrival.

Though these tribes continue to exist outside the borders of Guyana, their numbers are negligible. It is probable that they can neither harmonize with, nor master their environment. Without completely succumbing to the arguments of the environmental determinists, and the anthropogeographers in particular who argue that man's immediate environment is the all important factor in the evolution of his history, it must be admitted that its influence is considerable. Man and his environment do influence and react upon each other. It is hard to ignore Toynbee's 'challenge and response' theory which postulates that challenge there must be, as challenge stimulates survival and growth; nevertheless, the challenge must not be an impossibly unsurmountable one. One is therefore left with a mystery similar to that of the puzzling eclipse of the Mayas of the Old Empire Period, AD 800-925. In the unravelling of such mysteries, one speaks from varying degrees of ignorance. Evans and Meggers observed that the history of the origin and decline of a number of our Amerindian tribes had yet to be thoroughly investigated; their findings, they admitted, had but touched the surface. As regards the present tribes in the Guyana territory today, the Caribs, Arawaks, Warraus, and Wapisianas, the Akawois, Arecunas, Patamonas, Macusis, and Wai-Wais, there is no mystery about the increase of their numbers. From an approximate number of 7463 given in the 1891 census, the number increased to 31,000 in 1965 as noted in the Knapp Report. The health schemes, implemented by the Guyana government and helped by the missionaries, have produced remarkable results. The last census taken on 7 April 1970 listed the Amerindians at 32,794. It is estimated that this number has since increased to almost 40,000. The increase of these tribes in the twentieth century indeed vindicates Schomburgk's constant pleas that the indigenous race be preserved.

To Robert Schomburgk, that intrepid traveller, and to the young artist, E. A. Goodall, we owe a debt of gratitude for the vignettes of the lives of these interesting and fascinating tribes who, of all our people, can rightly claim to be the earliest, if not the original, inhabitants.

KEY TO REFERENCES

B—Barrington Brown, C. *Canoe and Camp Life in British Guiana*.

BIM—Brett, Revd W. H. *Indian Missions in Guiana*.

BIT—Brett, Revd W. H. *The Indian Tribes of Guiana*.

GED—Goodall's Expedition Diary in *Journal of the British Guiana Museum and Zoo*. No. 36 (31 December 1962), 47–64.

GGD—Goodall's Georgetown Diary in *Journal of the British Guiana Museum and Zoo*. No. 35 (30 September 1962), 39–53.

H—Hilhouse, William. *Indian Notices . . .* and 'Book of Reconnaissances . . .'

imT—im Thurn, Sir Everard F. *Among the Indians of Guiana*.

LG—*Local Guide of British Guiana containing Historical Sketches, Statistical Tables and the entire Statute Law of the Colony in force January 1, 1843*. Section 21.

M.C.P.—Minutes of the Court of Policy, British Guiana.

RC, 1790—Report of the Commissioners, W. A. van Sirtema van Grovestins and W. C. Boey to the Prince of Orange on the Condition of the Colony of Essequibo and Demerara, 27 July 1790 in *U.S. Commission on Boundary between Venezuela and British Guiana*. Vol. II. Extracts from the Archives. (Washington, 1897), 603.

R—Rodway, James. *The West Indies and the Spanish Main*.

SRi, I or II—Schomburgk, Richard. *Travels in British Guiana, 1840-1844*. 2 vols.

SRo—Schomburgk, Robert. *Description of British Guiana* and *Travels in the Interior of British Guiana, 1835-1839*.

THE PLATES
AND NOTES

The Warraus
'They inhabit the swampy district so often
mentioned, and, being near the sea, are excellent
fishermen, and subsist much upon the productions
of the waters. They cultivate cassava and other
vegetables, but do not pay sufficient attention to
agriculture, and, in times of scarcity betake
themselves to the ita palms, which abound in the
swamps. This tree is of the greatest service to
them. They are fond of its fruit, and at certain
seasons make of its pith a substitute for bread,
while its trunk is sometimes split and used in
flooring their dwellings, and its leaf supplies the
fibrous material of which, among other useful
things, they make strong and serviceable
hammocks, which form an important article in
their little traffic.

They are also noted for making canoes, with
which they supply the whole colony, the Arawaks
sometimes undertaking long voyages to their
remote settlements, and bringing the canoes, to
be again sold to the settlers, or disposed of among
themselves'.   Brett, W. H., *The Indian Tribes
of Guiana*, pp. 165-6.

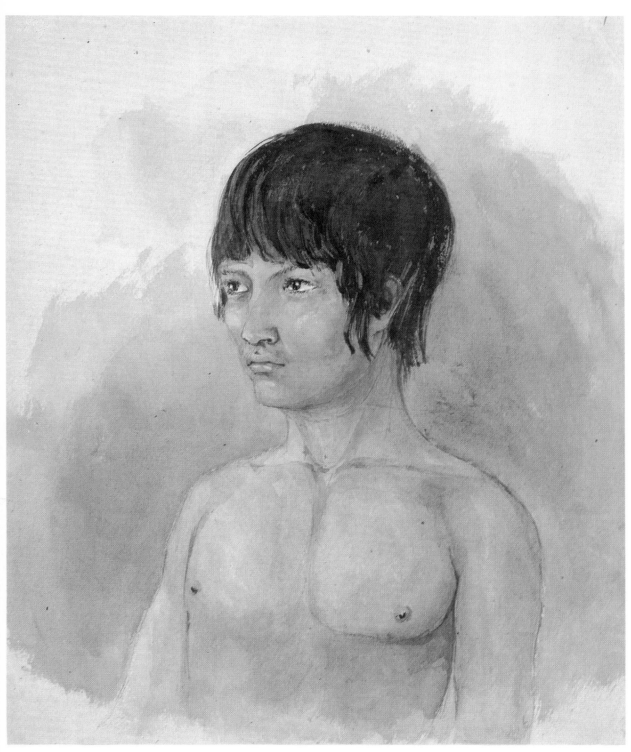

I A WARRAU ABOUT 16 YEARS

2

2 FRANCISCO—A CARIBISCI
3 FEMALES OF THE CARIBISI TRIBE

The Caribs

'The cloth which is worn by the Caribi men, secured by a cord round the loins, is often of sufficient length to form a kind of scarf. As it would otherwise trail on the ground they dispose it in a graceful manner over the shoulders, so that part of it falls on the bosom, while the end hangs down the back. It is often adorned with large cotton tassels, and is the most decent and serviceable, as well as the most picturesque covering worn by any of the native tribes. The coronal of feathers for the head is sometimes worn, but not generally. The head is usually adorned by a large daub of arnotto on the hair above the brow, and the forehead and cheeks are painted in various patterns with the same vermilion colour. This renders them ferocious in their appearance, and was probably adopted by their ancestors with that view, but the modern Caribs have an idea that it adds greatly to the beauty of their faces. Some men of this tribe also smear their bodies with the arnotto, in the manner already mentioned as practised by the women'. Brett, W. H., *The Indian Tribes of Guiana*, pp. 122-3.

The Caribs

'Their dress was merely a narrow strip of blue cloth, and their naked bodies were smeared with the red arnotto, which gave them the appearance of bleeding from every pore. As if this were not sufficiently ornamental, some of them had endeavoured to improve its appearance by blue spots upon their bodies and limbs. They wore round each leg, just below the knee, a tight strap of cotton, painted red, and another above each ankle. These are fastened on while the girl is young, and hinder the growth of the parts by their compression, while the calf which is unconfined, appears, in consequence, unnaturally large. All the Caribi women wear these, which they call sapuru, and consider as a great addition to their beauty. But the most singular part of their appearance is presented by the lower lip, which they perforate, and wear one, two, or three pins sticking through the hole, with the points outward. Before they procured pins, thorns or other similar substances were thus worn. Should they wish to use the pin, they will take it out, and again replace it in the lip when its services are no longer required'.
Brett, W. H., *The Indian Tribes of Guiana*, pp. 121-2.

5

4 A CARIBISI WOMAN
5 TUNA-WOYAI—A MACUSI CAPTAIN

The Caribs
'The nation of the Caribs . . . are looked upon as
nobles among the Indians. It is a very good thing
to have them as allies or friends, for they render
excellent services, but they are formidable
enemies, capable of more bravery and resistance
than one would think'.   van's Gravesande,
     Laurens Storm. *The Rise of British Guiana*,
                    pp. 598-9.

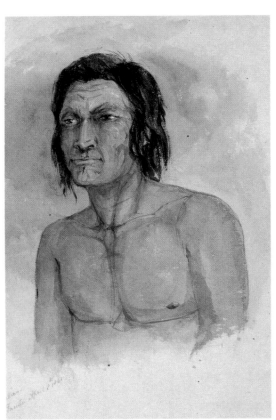

7

6 A MACUSI PLAYING THE QUAMA
7 A MACUSI INDIAN—RIVER TACUTU
8 WORO-KOMI—A MACUSI GIRL FROM AWARRA

8

9 ARUWAYARI—A MACUSI
10 MACUSI HUTS AT THE WOOD CAMASSARIN
    NEAR PIRARA

10

11

11 BASIKO—CHIEFTAIN OF THE MACUSIS
12 TAKUIBA—WORKING AT THE MOSA (HEIGHT
4 FT 11 INS)

The Macusis
'... the Macusis are one of the most numerous
and powerful tribes in British Guiana, that they
occupy the savannahs between the Rupununi,
Parima, along the Pacaraima and Canuku Ranges
to the number of about 1,500 souls, their whole
membership possibly amounting to about 3,000,
and that they are noted for their peace-loving,
complaisant, gentle and friendly character, but
especially for their love of order and cleanliness'.
Schomburgk, Richard, *Travels in
British Guiana 1840-1844*, Vol. 2, p. 246.

The Macusis
'Without doubt the Macusis, whose district
includes the savannahs of the Rupununi, the
Parima, and the mountain chains of the Pacaraima
and Canuku, belong to the most beautiful tribes
of Guiana, just as they likewise constitute at the
present time one of its most numerous ones. ...
The men wear their hair almost always short, the
women on the contrary having it nicely tidied and
hanging down over the neck and shoulders or else
rolled together in long plaits wound on top of the
head. Their speech is something unusually
euphonious and has much resemblance to French,
the largest number of their words ending in
-ong, -eng, or -ang. That they are an unusually
peaceable tribe is already confirmed by the
circumstance that all the slave raids by the Caribs
and other tribes were made in the territory of the
Macusis, as in more recent times similar raids
were made by the Brazilians. Peaceable and
harmless as is the tribe, it showed itself equally as
obliging, hospitable, and industrious during our
lengthy stay in its settlements, and it possesses one
rare superiority shared by only a few others, its
great love of order and cleanliness. Polygamy is
certainly practised, though one finds it but very
rarely. They also colour their face and body
thickly with Bignonia Chica and Genipa
Americana paint; the women, who are not less
indifferent to finery, particularly do this and try to
increase their natural beauty as much as possible
by external artificial means, in which connection
they set an especially high value upon their long
and beautiful black hair which one always finds
cleanly combed and anointed with crab oil. Their
ear lobes and, among the men, the nasal septum,
were bored. In the holes the men wore the
finger-long round little bits of stick or thin pieces
of cane, and I noticed among both sexes, without
exception, a small round opening in the under
lip through which, as in the case of the Caribs, a
pin with the tip outside was stuck. Several women
wore gold coins on their bead necklaces, a
demonstration that they knew the value of money
a little or not at all: amongst the coastal tribes one
might search in vain for such a decoration. The
apron-belts (Mosa) of the women consisted of a
sort of bead embroidery, with pretty angular
figures a la Grec, which had some resemblance to
those hieroglyphics that we found in Waraputa.
These aprons seemed to be their greatest pride,
just as they also constituted their chief finery'.
Schomburgk, Richard, *Travels in British
Guiana 1840-1844*, Vol. 1, pp. 280-1.

13

13 PARO—A MACUSI GIRL FROM AWARRA
14 AIYUKANTEE—A TEHWEKYE

14

15

16

15 PURREKA—A MACUSI FROM NAPPI PLAYING
   KAIKARA
16 NO CAPTION—INDIAN WITH HEAD FEATHERS
17 YAPOYARE—MACUSI MODE OF PADDLING CANOE
18 NO CAPTION—INDIAN WITH HEAD-DRESS AND
   BEADS
19 NO CAPTION—INDIAN WITH FACE MARKINGS

18

17

19

20 NO CAPTION—INDIAN WITH HEAD-DRESS,
    BLOW PIPE, ETC., AND DOG IN INDIAN HUT
21 NO CAPTION—INTERIOR OF HUT WITH INDIANS
    AND UTENSILS

21

22

23

22 INTERIOR OF CIRCULAR MACUSI HUT
23 INTERIOR OF A MACUSI HUT

The Maiongkongs

'... Maiongkongs, a tribe occupying the watershed of the upper Orinoco and its tributary, the Parima'.

'They were a big and finely developed people, the greater number of whom measured from 5ft. 6 inches to 8 inches, their body at the same time appearing more compact and muscular and their facial features more rounded than those of the other tribes hitherto known to me. The forehead was small and receding, while the eyes which lay close to each other, were more obliquely slit, and shaded with long eye-lashes; eyebrows and beard were depilated. Just as with the Caribs the objectionable custom of tying tight bandages above and below the calves of the little girls immediately after birth so as to force the latter to an artificial overgrowth only prevails among the women, it was practised here by the Maiongkong men whose muscles of the upper arm were at the same time swollen to an unnatural size by similar ligatures. Instead of the necklaces and beaded-strings on the ankles and upper arms the women wore cords plaited out of human hair, a material that the men twined round their loins like thick waist-belts, to which the apron was attached. The thicker such a belt (Matupa) the more surely did it bear witness to the courage of the wearer because the hair of fallen enemies is only employed in its manufacture. The aprons of the women were made of cotton fringes and were generally coloured red. The men's elegant feather decorations consisted for the greatest part of thick head-fillets of the red and yellow feathers which the Rhamphastos erythrorhynchos and R. vitellinus grow immediately above the root of the tail'. Schomburgk, Richard, *Travels in British Guiana 1840-1844*, Vol. I, pp. 315-16.

The Maiongkongs

'They [the Maiongkong] are a proud and haughty tribe. The Maiongkong continually struts about with a self-consciousness as if the whole world were subordinate to him. . . . He accordingly exercises extreme care over his appearance and parts his hair with the greatest exactness over his forehead'.

'The Maiongkong are excellent boat-builders and complete their work with fire and axe in a shorter time than any other Indians'.

Schomburgk, Robert, *Travels in the Interior of British Guiana, 1835-1839*, pp. 165, 168

24

25

26

24 A MAIONGKONG INDIAN FROM THE UPPER
   ORINOCO
25 AN ARECUNA—OUR GUIDE TO THE CUYUNI
26 AN ARECUNA

The Arecunas
'The Arekunas are evidently a brother tribe of the
Macusis: language, manners and customs
apparently correspond with one another. . . .
Almost all the men wear the hair-belt (Matupa)
over the hips, some also have a belt manufactured
of spun cotton something after the style of a
sausage: the women have necklaces made of the
teeth of small rodents. The blow gun . . . appears
to be their chief weapon. . . . Their chieftains exert
greater influence and power than do the
Macusis. . . . The Arekunas are only in direct
relations with Georgetown through exchanging
spun cotton, hammocks, dogs, and feather
decorations for small articles of European manufacture with the Akawais who are not afraid of the
dangerous journey up the Cuyuni or Mazaruni . . .'.
      Schomburgk, Richard, *Travels in British
            Guiana 1840-1844*, Vol. 2, p. 189.

27

27 ARECUNA
28 A BOY OF THE ARECUNA TRIBE

The Arecunas

'The latter [the Arecunas] whom we had not seen
before, had journeyed from the high lands between
the heads of the Cuyuni and the Caroni, a large
tributary of the Orinoco. They had come from
thence to the head of the Waini, where they had
cut down some large trees and made 'wood-skin'
canoes, as they are called. These wood-skins are
formed by stripping off the bark of the mariwayani,
or purple-heart, in one large piece, forcing it open
in the middle, and fixing sticks across it :–
downward slits being cut near the extremities,
which are supported on beams till the bark be
dry, to give them a slight spring above the surface
of the water. In those frail barks they had
descended the Waini, and come through the
connecting streams to our mission.

Those strangers were fine stalwart men, with
clear copper-tinted skins, and larger in person
than the Indians near the coast. Though not greatly
encumbered with clothing, they possessed
unusual attractions in the way of ornament. They
wore long sticks through the cartilage of the
nostrils, and had still longer ones, very handsomely
adorned with tufts of black feathers at the
extremities, fixed through their ears. Evidently
they were most attentive to their personal
appearance, and they made a great sensation. . . .
both sexes had their countenances much tattooed,
and those facial ornaments were, of course,
indelible. Some of the women had the dark blue
lines traced across the upper lip, and extending in
wavy curves over either cheek, resembling
immense curled moustachios ; but the favourite
style seemed to be a broad line round the mouth,
so wide that each lip appeared to be an inch
broader, and the aperture itself two inches longer
than nature had made it'.   Brett, W. H., *The
Indian Tribes of Guiana*, pp. 267-8.

28

29

29 CAMP NEAR THE MOUTH OF THE PIRARA
30 TWO INDIAN HUTS

30

33

32

31 WAI-I-PARI—CHIEF OF WATU-TICABA
32 WAPISIANA FROM WATU-TICABA
33 KIWI-ISK-TEHRK—A WAPISIANA FROM
PINIGHETTE

The Wapisianas
'I had already enjoyed many an opportunity for
admiring the hair of Indian women, but I had
never yet seen it in such length and profusion as
possessed by the Wapisianas. They generally had
it nicely smoothed, tidied up and greased with
palm oil: falling over the shoulders, it reached to
the calves in many cases. The men almost always
cut theirs short. In the perforated nasal septum
they (men) wore polished smooth and flattened-
out silver or copper coins, and in the perforated
under lip either a small cylinder or sort of bell
made of bone. In their clothing, the men and
women corresponded with other tribes, in that it
consisted only of a lap-cloth'.
    Schomburgk, Richard, *Travels in British
        Guiana 1840-1844*, Vol. 2, pp. 31-2.

The Wapisianas
'The Wapisianas are more athletic, and darker in
colour than the Macusis. Their females are often
good-looking, and stain and puncture the skin
round the mouth in an elliptical form. Their
language is very peculiar, and stands isolated
among those of the tribes who dwell near them'.
    Brett, W. H., *The Indian Tribes of Guiana*, p. 498.

34

34 A WAPISIANA ABOUT 18 YEARS (JIM)
35 POATIRRK—A WAPISIANA FROM WATU-TICABA
36 NO CAPTION—THREE AMERINDIANS IN A HUT

35

Caripu d. Atorai

Atorai

38

37 CARIPU—AN ATORAI
38 AKHARI-KHURRU—AN ATORAI

The Atorais
'The Atorais are now nearly extinct. Including a
sister tribe, the Tauris or Dauris, who formerly
dwelt apart in the forests, but are not united with
them, the Atorais probably do not exceed one
hundred persons. They appear to have been the
only tribe in Guiana who have burnt their dead
upon a funeral pile. Their language differs
materially from that of the Wapisianas, and those
of the other neighbouring tribes'.

Brett, W. H., *The Indian Tribes of Guiana*, p. 498.

39

40

39 ERUSUMARITAI—A TAYRAI
40 HIRAWAPA—A TAURAI
41 AKHARI-KHURRU—AN ATORAI

Drawn by C.H. Jordan

Akkari Khurru a Atooai

42

42 INDIAN HUTS
43 MIAHA-AN AMARIPA—LAST OF HER TRIBE
44 KARA—WATYA, A TARUMA

43

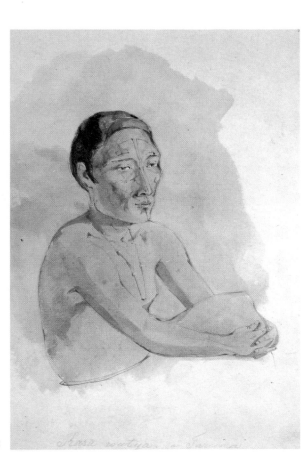

44

The Amaripas
'. . . another who especially attracted our attention among the Indians flocking around was an aged woman, "the last of her race", a striking picture of human frailty and decay. . . . Miaha seemed to be about 60 years of age. Neither the grief over her tribesmen who had gone before, nor the succession of years that had passed over her had been able to bleach her long hair: with the same fulness as in her youth it still covered the now more gaunt nape and fleshless shoulders while it lent a peculiar expression to the hoary and venerable face with its markedly curved aquiline nose'.

Schomburgk, Richard, *Travels in British Guiana 1840-1844*, Vol. 2, pp. 308-9.

46

47

The Tarumas

'They [the Tarumas] occupied the upper
Essequibo with its tributaries the Cuyuwini and
the Yuawauri. According to some mysterious
legends, they appear to have formerly occupied
the Rio Negro. A portion of them were there
converted by the Portuguese missions, while
another felt compelled on that account to shift
their old quarters to follow the banks of the rivers
which arise in the Sierra Acarai and settle at the
sources of the Essequibo. Among those that were
converted, who stayed behind on the Rio Negro,
death raged so violently that they soon died out,
on which account von Martius, to whom the other
portion of the tribe remained unknown, regarded
the Tarumas as already extinct. . . . With the
exception of a smaller head, they entirely corresponded in physical conformation with remaining
tribes of Indians, but they varied all the more
from them not only in language but especially in
the pronunciation of words. The Tarumas are
held in high repute among the tribes of the interior
for the excellent training of their hunting dogs.
Their apron belts and graters are also celebrated'.
Schomburgk, Richard, *Travels in British
Guiana 1840-1844*, Vol. 2, p. 309.

The Tarumas

'The Tarumas formerly lived near the mouth of
the Rio Negro. The Carmelites had a Mission
among them as early as 1670. Disagreeing with
other tribes, and being ill-used by the
Portuguese, a portion of them fled northward, and
settled near the head waters of the Essequibo.
Death made such ravages among those who
remained, that the tribe was considered extinct.
Mahanarva, the well-known Caribi chief, brought
the first information of their existence to Demerara,
but his account was so exaggerated that they were
described as amphibious, and taking shelter in
caverns under water. They are about four hundred
in number, and their language differs from that
of the other Indians of Guiana'.
Brett, W. H., *Indian Missions in Guiana*, p. 300.

Drawn by E. L. Goodee

48

49

50

48 NO CAPTION—INDIAN WITH GUN
49 PAKE-SIKO—A TARUMA WOMAN
50 MAN-TYATOCKO—A MAOPITYAN

The Maopityans

'The latter [the Maopityans] differed essentially both in build of body and in attire from all other Indians that my brother had become acquainted with during the course of his travels. Although their height quite corresponded with the other Indians, their figure if more slender was nevertheless more bony than that of the Tarumas. Their head was compressed laterally, and their facial expression, on account of the lustrous eyes, brighter. They wore their hair tied up into a long tail carried in a 10 to 12 inch sort of cone made of palm-leaves from which a number of strings with the most variegated feather-attachments fell dependent'.

'The total number of still living Maopityans amounted to 39, who together with some 20 Tarumas from whom they had chosen their chief, occupied the two houses. They call themselves Mawakwas, but the Wapisianas call them Maopityans from Mao, the frog and Pityan, the people or tribe'.   Schomburgk, Richard, *Travels in British Guiana 1840-1844*, Vol. 2, pp. 376, 378.

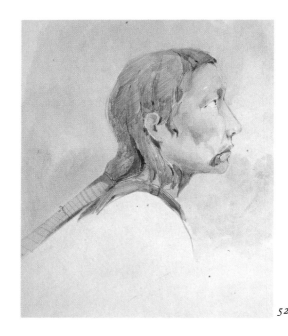

51

52

51 A MAOPITYAN
52 A MAOPITYAN
53 A MAOPITYAN WOMAN
54 A YOUNG FEMALE OF THE MAOPITYAN
55 A MAOPITYAN—OUR GUIDE TO CUTARI

The Maopityans

'... one a Maopityan or Frog Indian, who differed
from the rest, and other Guiana tribes, in the shape
of his head, which was exceedingly long, narrow,
and high, and had a most extraordinary
appearance. This form of head is a manufactured
one, being produced by the application of two
flat pieces of wood to the sides of the head of the
infant Maopityan immediately after its birth.
There the wood is firmly bound until the head
becomes flattened at its sides, and of course
heightened at the top. This is somewhat similar to
the custom of the flat-head Indians of North
America, differing only in the application of the
boards to the sides, instead of to the front and
back of the head'.   Barrington Brown, C.,
Canoe and Camp Life in British Guiana, pp. 246-7.

53

54

55

57

58

59

56 A MAOPITYAN OR MAWAIKO IN HIS DANCING
DRESS
57 ARARIKA—A MAOPITYAN
58 TSHU-KUCKU—A MAOPITYAN WITH SUCKLING
BABY
59 A YOUNG MAOPITYAN WOMAN

60

60 A MAOPITYAN HUT
61 THE MAOPITYAN HUT-PEOPLE, HAMMOCKS
AND HUT DESIGN

Maopityan Huts
'They [Robert Schomburgk, Goodall and Indian
guides] crossed Mt Kenukawai and reached the
Valley of the Darura, the first tributary of note of
the Caphiwuin. After an uninterrupted march of
5 miles they arrived at the provision fields of the
Maopityan settlement, which consisted of two
large bee-hive houses: on the tops of these there
rose a second smaller bee-hive roof from which
hung several flat pieces of wood shaped into all
kinds of figures that were swayed backwards and
forwards by the wind. It was only with fear and
trembling that the women ventured to put out
their hands to welcome the newcomers. The two
houses lodged the last remnant of the once
powerful tribe of the Maopityans or Frog Indians.

The larger of the houses with a height of 100 feet,
and a diameter of 86, had at its centre a strong
post which they called Aiyukuba: it was covered
with a quantity of Indian figures and
hieroglyphics'.   Schomburgk, Richard, *Travels
in British Guiana 1840-1844*, Vol. 2, p. 377.

62

62 A CHIEFTAIN OF THE PIANOGHOTTOS
63 A PIANOGHOTTO BOY
64 A PIANOGHOTTO INDIAN FROM UPPER CUTARI

63

The Pianoghottos
'... half an hour later they reached a Pianoghotto
village where they were awaited and welcomed by
the athletic and well-built inhabitants. In their
costume they quite resembled the Maopityans:
indeed so much care had been spent on the pig-tail
that it would have done credit to the most
fashionable Parisian hairdresser. The body was
not decorated in lines, but with the exception of
the face, was painted red from chin to toe. The
men wore plenty of beads around the loins and
shoulders and like the Zurumatas, below the knees
cotton strings from which a number of tassels
were dependent. Around the neck of each man a
prettily made comb hung down upon the breast.
The bows and arrows were unusually long: they
did not possess war clubs. The women were far
more niggardly fleshed by Nature than the men
and wore their hair cropped quite short'.
Schomburgk, Richard, *Travels in British
Guiana 1840-1844*, Vol. 2, p. 383.

The Drios
'. . . close to the sources of the Wanamu . . . the
Drios, a fellow-tribe of the Pianoghottos. . . .
Except that the Drios, like the South Sea Islanders,
tattoo the whole body, they exactly correspond
in build and attire with the Pianoghottos. . .'.
  Schomburgk, Richard, *Travels in British
Guiana 1840-1844*, Vol. 2, pp. 383-4.

65 A DRIO WOMAN FROM WENAMU
66 OF THE MIXED RACE—THE SON OF A NEGRO AND
   A WAPISIANA WOMAN

82

67

67 WAREHRE—SON OF A WAPISIANA WOMAN
68 MACUSI VILLAGE—TARONG YACUOISE

68

69 AKAWAIO HUT

SELECT BIBLIOGRAPHY

Published books

BARRINGTON BROWN, C. *Canoe and Camp Life in British Guiana*. London. Edward Stanford, 1876.

BENNETT, C. W. *Illustrated History of British Guiana*. Demerara. The Colonist Office, 1866.

BERNAU, Revd J. H. *Missionary Labours in British Guiana with Remarks on the Manners, Customs and Superstitious Rites of the Aborigines*. London. J. F. Shaw, 1847.

BODDAM-WHETHAM, J. W. *Roraima and British Guiana*. London. Hurst and Blackett, 1879.

BOLINGBROKE, Henry. *A Voyage to the Demerary, 1799-1806*. Guiana Edition, No. 1. Edited by Vincent Roth. Georgetown. The Daily Chronicle, 1947.

BRETT, Revd W. H. *Indian Missions in Guiana*. London. George Bell, 1851.

— *The Indian Tribes of Guiana: Their Condition and Habits*. London. Bell and Daldy, 1868.

— *Guiana Legends*. London. S.P.C.K., 1931.

BRONKHURST, H. V. P. *The Origin of the Guyanian Indians ascertained; or the Aborigines of America, (especially of the Guyanas) and the East Indian Coolie Immigrants compared*. Georgetown. The Colonist Office, 1881.

COUDREAU, O. *Voyage au Cumina, 20 April 1900-07*. Paris. A. Lature, 1907. Ch. XI 'The Piancoto', translated by W. E. Roth. The Roth Collection, University of Guyana Library.

DANCE, Revd C. *Guianese Log Book*. Georgetown. The Royal Gazette, 1881.

EVANS, Clifford and MEGGERS, Betty, J. *Archaeological Investigations in British Guiana*. Washington. U.S. Government Printing Office, 1960.

FARABEE, William Curtis. *The Central Arawaks*. Anthropological Publications, Oosterhout N.B., the Netherlands, 1967.

HANCOCK, Dr John. *Observations on the Climate, Soil, and Production of British Guiana, and on the Advantages of Emigration to and Colonizing the Interior of That Country*. 2nd edn. London. C. Richards, 1840.

HARTSINCK, Jan Jacob. *The Discovery of Guiana and Description of the Various European Possessions there*. Translated by Walter E. Roth from *Beschryving van Guiana*. 2 vols. Amsterdam, 1770. Ms. in University of Guyana Library.

HERDERSCHEE, A. Franssen. *Report of the Tapanahoni Expedition*. Translated by W. E. Roth, 1923. The Roth Collection, University of Guyana Library.

HILHOUSE, William. *Indian Notices, or Sketches of the Habits, Characters, Languages, Superstitions, Soil and Climate of the Several Nations; with Remarks on their capacity for colonization, present government, and suggestion for Future Improvement and Civilisation, also the Icthyology of the Fresh Waters of the Interior*. Published for the Author, Demerara, 1825.

IM THURN, Sir Everard F. *Among the Indians of Guiana*. London. Kegan Paul, Trench & Co., 1883; reprint Dover edn., New York, 1967.

— *On the Animism of the Indians of British Guiana*. London. Harrison and Sons, 1882.

— *Demerara Papers*. 'Indian Tribes of British Guiana 1878-79'.

KIRKE, Henry. *Twenty-five Years in British Guiana*. London. Sampson Low, Marston & Co., 1898.

MARRAT, Revd Jabez. *In the Tropics*. 2nd edn. London. Wesleyan Conference Office, 1881.

NETSCHER, P. M. *History of the Colonies, Essequibo, Demerary & Berbice. From the Dutch Establishment to the Present Day*. Translated by W. E. Roth. 'S Gravenhage. Martinus Nijhoff, 1888; reprint Georgetown. The Daily Chronicle, 1922.

PINCKARD, Dr George. *Letters from Guiana*. Extracted *Notes on the West Indies* . . . 1796-97. Edited by V. Roth. Georgetown. The Daily Chronicle, 1942.

RODWAY, James *The West Indies and the Spanish Main*. London. T. Fisher Unwin, 1896.

ROTH, Walter Edmund. *An Inquiry into the Animism and Folk Lore of the Guiana Indians*. Smithsonian Institution, Bureau of Ethnology. Washington, D.C. Government Printing Office, 1915.

— *An Introductory Study of the Arts, Crafts and Customs of the Guiana Indians*. Smithsonian Institution, Bureau of Ethnology. Washington, D.C. Government Printing Office, 1924.

— *Additional Studies of the Arts, Crafts and Customs of the Guiana Indians*. With special reference to those of southern British Guiana. Smithsonian Institution, Bureau of Ethnology. Washington, D.C. Government Printing Office, 1929.

SCHOMBURGK, Richard. *Travels in British Guiana, 1840-1844.* 2 vols. Translated and edited by W. E. Roth. Leipzig. J. J. Weber, 1848: reprint edn. Georgetown. The Daily Chronicle, 1922.

SCHOMBURGK, Sir Robert H. *A Description of British Guiana.* London. Simpkin, Marshall & Co., 1840: reprint edn. London. Frank Cass & Co., 1970.

— *Travels in the Interior of British Guiana, 1835–1839.* Leipzig. George Wigand, 1841: reprint edn. Georgetown. The Argosy Co. Ltd., 1931.

— *On the Natives of Guiana.* Paper read before the Royal Geographical Society, 27 November, 1844.

— (ed.) *Discovery of the Large, Rich and Beautiful Empire of Guiana.* London. Hakluyt Society, 1848.

ST CLAIR, Lt Staunton Thomas. *A Soldier's Sojourn in British Guiana, 1806-1808.* The Guiana Edition, No. 9. Edited by V. Roth. Georgetown: The Daily Chronicle, 1947.

STEDMAN, Captain J. G. *Narrative of a Five Years' Expedition against the Revolted Negroes of Surinam in Guiana, or the Wild Coast of South America from the year 1772 to 1777.* 2 vols. London. J. J. Johnson and J. Edwards, 1796: reprint edn. edited by R. A. J. van Lier. Massachusetts. University of Massachusetts Press, 1972.

VAN BERKEL, Adrian. *Travels in South America between the Berbice and Essequibo Rivers and in Surinam, 1670–1689.* Translated by W. E. Roth. The Guiana Edition, No. 2. Georgetown. The Daily Chronicle, 1948.

VAN'S GRAVESANDE, Laurens Storm. *The Rise of British Guiana.* Compiled from his despatches by C. A. Harris and J. A. J. Villiers. 2 vols. London. Hakluyt Society, 1911.

VENESS, Revd W. T. *El Dorado or British Guiana as a Field for Colonisation.* London. 1866. (n.p.)

WATERTON, Charles. *Wanderings in South America.* London. Macmillan & Co. Ltd., 1879.

WINTER, A. *Indian Pictured Rocks of Guiana (with a short Account of the Potaro Indian Mission).* London. Judd and Co., 1883.

Articles and Periodicals

BROWN, C. G. 'Indian Picture Writing in British Guiana', *Journal of Anthropological Institute of Great Britain and Ireland*, II (1872), 255-56.

COLTHURST, R. T. E. 'Our Amerindians of British Guiana', *Caribia*, VIII, 19.

GILLIN, John. 'Crime and Punishment among the Barama River Caribs of British Guiana', *American Anthropologist.* New Series, XXXVI (1934) 331-44.

— 'Social Life of the Barama River Caribs of British Guiana', *The Scientific Monthly*, XL (March 1935) 227-36.

HARPER, W. 'Tribes of British Guiana', *Anthropological Institute*, II (1873) 254-57.

HILHOUSE, William. 'Memoir in the Warrow Land of British Guiana', *Journal of the Royal Geographical Society*, IV (1834) 321-33.

— 'Notices of the Indians settled in the Interior of British Guiana', *Ibid.*, II (1832) 22-49.

— 'Book of Reconnaissances and Indian Miscellany, 1823', British Guiana Boundary. Appendix to the Case on Behalf of the Government of Her Britannic Majesty. VI, 22-33.

IM THURN, Sir Everard F. 'Measles and a Moral', *The West Indian Quarterly* (1887-88) 267.

KLOOS, Peter. 'Amerindians of Surinam', in Professor W. Dostal (ed.) *The Situation of the Indians in South America.* Geneva. World Council of Churches, 1972.

VENESS, Revd W. T. 'A Strange Delusion', *The West Indian Quarterly* No. 3 (July 1887) 93-102.

VON MARTIUS, Dr C. F. Ph. 'On the Aboriginal Inhabitants of Brazil', *Journal of the Royal Geographical Society*, II (1832).

Articles from TIMEHRI: The Journal of the Royal Agricultural and Commercial Society of British Guiana, 1882-1967.

ANTHON, Michael. 'The Kanaima', Fifth Series. XXXVI (October 1957).

BUTT, Audrey. 'The Burning Fountain from whence it came', Fifth Series. XXXIII (October 1954).

— 'Birth of a Religion', Fifth Series, XXXVII (September 1959).

'Couvade', No. 2a, II (December 1883).

'Couvade', No. 3a, III (December 1884).

DAVIS, N. Darnell. 'Beginnings of British Guiana', New Series, No. 12, VII (June 1893).

— 'Capitulation to the French in 1762', New Series, No. 11, VI (June 1892).

— 'Records of British Guiana', New Series, No. 7, 11 (June 1888).

DE LA BORDE, Pere. 'History of the Caribs', Translated by G. J. A. Boschreitz No. 5a, V (December 1886).

HARTSINCK, Jan Jacob. 'Indians of Guiana', Translated from the Dutch. New Series, No. 12, VII (June 1893).

IM THURN, Sir Everard F. 'Animism', No. 3a, III (December 1884).

— 'Essequibo, Demerara and Berbice under the Dutch', No. 2a, II (December 1883) and No. 3a, III (December 1884).

— 'Indian Privileges', No. 1, I (June 1882).

— 'Primitive Games', New Series, No. 8, III (June 1889).

— 'The Schomburgk Brothers', No. 3, III (June 1884).

— 'Tame Animals Among the Red Men of America', No. 1, I (December 1882).

— 'Red Men; some of their Thoughts', No. 5, V (June 1886).

LEIGH, Captain Charles. 'First English Colony in Guiana', New Series, No. 14 IX June 1895).

LICKERT, Revd S. J. 'Moruca', Third Series, No. 19, II (July 1912).

McCLINTOCK, W. C. H. F. 'Census of Indians of Pomeroon', No. 3a, III (December 1884).

— 'Colonial Jottings', No. 5a, V (December 1886).

— 'Spanish Arawaks of Morooka', No. 3, III (December 1884).

— 'An Accawoi Peiaiman', *Ibid*.

MEGGERS, Dr Betty and EVANS, Dr Clifford. 'Preliminary Results of Archaeological Investigation in British Guiana'. Fifth Series. No. 34 (September 1955).

PATERSON, John D. 'Crown Lands of British Guiana', No. 13a, VIII (December 1894).

POONAI, N. O. 'Extinct Tribes and Threatened Species of the South Savannahs', XLIII (January–December 1967).

QUELCH, J. J. 'Materials of Urali Poison', New Series, No. 14, IX (June 1895).

RODWAY, James. 'Constitution of British Guiana', New Series, No. 10a, V (December 1891).

— 'Indian Policy of the Dutch', New Series, No. 15, X (June 1896).

— 'Life History of an Indian', New Series, No. 13, VIII (June 1894).

— 'The Old Boundary of Essequibo', New Series, No. 14a, IX (December 1895).

— 'The Schomburgks in Guiana', New Series, No. 8, III (June 1889).

— 'Schomburgkiana', New Series, No. 15, X (June 1896).

— 'Scraps of Indian Folk-lore', New Series, No. 12, VII (June 1893).

— 'Timehri, or Pictured Rocks', Third Series. No. 23, VI (September 1919).

ROTH, Vincent. 'Amerindian and the State', Fifth Series. No. 31, (November 1952).

— 'Hilhouse's Book of Reconnaissances and Indian Miscellany', Fourth Series. No. 25 (December 1934).

ROWLAND, Dr E. D. 'Census of British Guiana', New Series. No. VI (June 1892).

WILLIAMS, Revd James. 'Americans of the Interior of British Guiana', Third Series. No. 19, II (July 1912).

— 'Indian Languages', Third Series. No. 21, IV (June 1917).

WOOD, B. R. 'Curare', Fifth Series. No. 26 (November 1944).

YDE, Dr Jens. 'Agricultural Level of the Wai-Wai Indians', Fifth Series. No. 36 (October 1957).

CONCORDANCE

Frontispiece	Add. Mss. 16939, f. 1.	Plate 24	Add. Mss. 16937, f. 5.	Plate 48	Add. Mss. 16937, f. 61.
Plate 1	16937, f. 1.	25	16937, f. 34.	49	16937, f. 59.
2	16937, f. 2.	26	16937, f. 32.	50	16937, f. 63.
3	16937, f. 3.	27	16937, f. 35.	51	16937, f. 64.
4	16937, f. 4.	28	16937, f. 31.	52	16937, f. 66.
5	16937, f. 8.	29	16939, f. 13.	53	16937, f. 70.
6	16937, f. 10.	30	16939, f. 17.	54	16937, f. 67.
7	16937, f. 7.	31	16937, f. 37.	55	16937, f. 68.
8	16937, f. 9.	32	16937, f. 38.	56	16937, f. 72.
9	16937, f. 14.	33	16937, f. 40.	57	16937, f. 69.
10	16939, f. 14.	34	16937, f. 43.	58	16937, f. 71.
11	16937, f. 17.	35	16937, f. 42.	59	16937, f. 65.
12	16937, f. 21.	36	16937, f. 46.	60	16938, f. 14.
13	16937, f. 11.	37	16937, f. 48.	61	16939, f. 24.
14	16937, f. 12.	38	16937, f. 50.	62	16937, f. 74.
15	16937, f. 24.	39	16937, f. 49.	63	16937, f. 75.
16	16937, f. 27.	40	16937, f. 51.	64	16937, f. 76.
17	16937, f. 20.	41	16937, f. 52.	65	16937, f. 77.
18	16937, f. 28.	42	16936, f. 76.	66	16937, f. 83.
19	16937, f. 30.	43	16937, f. 53.	67	16937, f. 80.
20	16937, f. 29.	44	16937, f. 56.	68	16936, f. 10.
21	16939, f. 22.	45	16939, f. 18.	69	16936, f. 78.
22	16939, f. 19.	46	16937, f. 57.		
23	16939, f. 21.	47	16937, f. 58.		

ACKNOWLEDGEMENTS

For biographical details on the life of the artist, Edward Alfred Goodall, acknowledgements are made to the correspondence between the Honourable Vincent Roth, Curator of the British Guiana Museum and Zoo, 1962, and the artist's grandson, Mr E. A. Goodall of British Columbia. This correspondence was made available through the courtesy of Mr G. Burnham, the present Curator of the Guyana Museum. Other biographical notes and references were obtained from Nos. 35 and 36 of the *Journal of the British Guiana Museum and Zoo, 1962*; *Who Was Who, 1897-1915*; Christopher Wood, *Dictionary of Victorian Painters*, and the *Espasa Calpe Encyclopaedia*.

Grateful thanks to Mrs Brigid Harrington, Bibliographer/Librarian of the Institute of Latin American Studies, University of London, for checking biographical material for me, to Mrs I. Beharry, Secretary, St Joseph High School, Guyana, for helping to type the script, and to my colleagues on the National Commission for Research Materials, Guyana, for their valuable comments on the script. Above all, I wish to record my gratitude to the Minister of Information and Culture, Guyana, for her whole-hearted encouragement and generous assistance without which this work would not have been published.